# Married: But It Can Happen

R. Y. Burgess

This book is dedicated to my 3 amazing children;

Me'Kayla, Michelle and my baby sweet baby boy

Micah!

## Introduction

The 1980s was right when the street dancers began being big and movies like Beat Street and Breakin' were giving people with dreams a reason to not give up on them. That time period was also when I was born, April 22, 1983 to be exact. My mom says that when she had me she went right into a coma for a few days. When she finally came alert and they brought her to me she said, "Whose baby is this? That's not my baby that's a Chinese lady's baby!" Luckily for me she had no choice but to know I was her daughter since I was the only girl born at Baptist Hospital that night. After 8 years of trying to have another child I was finally born into this world and ready to conquer it, but first I had to endure a few obstacles.

Do you know what it feels like to be called Roger Rabbit, Bugs Bunny, Rat, or any name to anything that had big teeth? Well I do, after second grade that was all I heard never heard my name called much. Lots of kids thought my big bucked-teeth were naturally there but let me tell you they were not. February 14 in second grade is what made my third through eleventh grade years the worst ever. I was swinging in between two desks and my hands slipped and my feet came from under me and I fell flat on my face. I knocked out one tooth and chipped the other tooth. I had to be rushed to the dentist and the severity of my damages caused them to cancel all scheduled appointments for that day. They were able to save one tooth and had to rebuild the other tooth. As a result this surgery left me bucked-teeth and the pretty, cavity free smile I so proudly carried was gone and I now had this smile that I didn't want to show. I'd take pictures and not part my lips at all. What hurt the most was that those who were in my second grade class and followed me in middle and high school knew what happened and still joined in on the name calling. So at the age of 7 I had to learn to be strong.

Middle school was also when I met Crucial Conflict; Crucial Conflict was a 90's hip hop group from Chicago, known for their 'rodeo' style and their hit song "Hay (in the Middle of the Barn)".They came to our school and performed for the after school Teams Program. I remember when this girl sat in class and peed during a test because she was afraid to miss the test. I also remember this girl I almost fought for my cousin over a Ray J poster. Oh, the things we would have done for our family in school and outside of school. Those were the good old years but the best was yet to come. In eighth grade I joined my middle school band and learned first to play the French horn and I didn't like it so I switched to the Clarinet. This was an instrument I loved and I mastered the art of playing this instrument! I had a gift I didn't realize I had and still do and that's a love and passion for music.

While in middle school in eighth grade I also

learned another new skill and that was the World Wide Web. Yahoo became my portal to the outside world. I will never forget my first internet stop to the Rap chat rooms. I use to go in there and battle who ever wanted some. My rap name then was Rated-R and after I got tired of that chat I went over to R&B chat. The first person I met was Johnny aka Seige. We grew a great bond and to this day I can truly say I love him. I also met many other's… boy so many of you all I can't list all of you. From 1997 until about 2006 I was on chatting hard. I learned how to hack, boot, and run some powerful programs. I love all of those who I have grown a great bond with from chat and I consider them apart of my life always. I even did a little bit of internet dating. Obviously it didn't work but it was fun and a great learning experience. Not only was I observed going from child to adult in folks faces but also on the internet. Thanks Bill Gates!

It’s funny how you remember the things that hurt you most rather than things that gave you the greatest joys. Elementary, Middle, and High School all gave me good and bad memories but the worst of all was the thing I had to endure at the age of 24.

## FROM TEEN TO YOUNG ADULT

You almost never forget the first person you had sex with or made love to, and they never forget you. 'Big Peter' is what I called him, although Peter wasn't his real name. He was tall, slim, and light-skinned, just like I liked them. It was the summer before my 9th grade year and I was at my Grandma Jack's house that whole summer. I was 14 years old that summer, and Master P was on a come up with No Limit Records, plus the movie *Bout It, Bout It* had come out. I was at a friend's house watching it in the neighborhood my grandmother lived. One thing led to another, and I found myself at his house, in his bed, and engaged in things I had never before done....My mom is--- shoot, my mom *and* dad are probably going to kill me when they read this. But, hey, I'm grown with 3 kids. Love you (smile)!

Sure, I had kissed boys before. But here I was, naked and about to let this boy inside of me. After about five to ten minutes I started bleeding, and there you have it: he popped my cherry. I had heard about it, but seeing it and feeling it I got hysterical; I jumped up and put on my clothes and I left. He tried to get me to come back days later, but I was so embarrassed and scared that I ignored him. I didn't see him again until the first day of school. He was in the 11th grade then, and we spoke, but that was about it. The next time I saw him anywhere was when I was going back and forth to have stress tests done before giving birth to my oldest daughter in 2003. I had no more sex after that until I met 'the sperm donor'...

"I still can't believe it!" I said to myself as I stood in the hallway of the Jacksonville Coliseum. Today was graduation day for the Class of 2000 of William M. Raines Sr. High School. I was 17 years old and about to embark on a journey into the real world.

Graduating one year early made me feel like I was the smartest in the world. Of course I knew that I wasn't, but why not feel special like that on this day? As I walked across that stage I was nervous, shaking, and praying to God I didn't trip in these shoes I had on; I hated wearing heels, but I had them on for this occasion. I can say this though: I felt *so* out of place at graduation. Even though I knew almost everyone I was around, I felt like maybe I was moving too fast; like maybe I should wait and graduate with the class of 2001. "Oh well. I'm here now, so let's get this over with", I said to myself, as I got up and got in line to get my diploma. That night, after all of that was over, I went out and celebrated.

Realizing that I was now considered an adult, I did what most adults do: I got a job! My first job was doing surveys at the Regency Square Mall. Of course, this was when the mall was thick and packed every day of the week. I met so many people while doing that job that when they saw me outside work they spoke.

I also remember working for Convergys Corp, which I can't even count how many people have worked for them. I loved the job, but I hated calling people's homes. I was doing outbound calls trying to sell consumers AT&T Long Distance Service. That was the same time I met the second boyfriend I ever had, JW. He lived in Mobile, Alabama--- well, 'eight-mile' Alabama, but it's right there. I was so head-over-heels in love with this boy. I had, by then, been fired from Convergys. They said I wasn't on the phones enough; I was gone off the lines for more than 15 minutes. I couldn't help the fact that their bathrooms were only on the 2nd and 3rd floors! My desk was on the 1st floor! I guess they wanted me to skip wiping my behind and washing my hands. Oh well… I ended up getting hired at Winn Dixie grocery store. I worked there until July 4th of whatever year that was. While working at Winn Dixie, I decided I would just up and move to Alabama with JW. His mom had given the ok, BUT my parents had no idea. I guess I had one of those I'm-grown-and-I-can-do-what-I-want attitudes. Technically I was grown, but I didn't know I had so much more growing up to do. So I decided one day that, instead of going to work, I would dress as if I was headed to work and, instead, drive all the way to Mobile, Alabama. Once I got there, I finally met his mom face-to-face, and then went to the mall to get myself some clothes and stuff, because I didn't bring anything with me at all. Once I didn't come home that evening, my parents figured out I went to Alabama and called his mom's house asking me to come back home. So, the next morning, I was on the road back to Jacksonville. I left behind the things I had bought, not realizing that I was probably never going to see them again. That same trip I got my first speeding ticket ever in Madison County, and I learned that I would never fly through that county ever again.

The year was now 2002, and I was finally about to take my first semester of college classes at FCCJ. Unfortunately, I failed that first semester with all F's because I was doing everything but focusing on school. Back in 2001, after breaking up with my military boyfriend that I worked with at Sears, I met this really tall, handsome guy. I had been working at Sears Auto Center and, while out to lunch one day, I went to Burger King. Sitting there eating lunch was him. He was on his lunch break, and he asked me to sit for a few and have lunch with him, so I did. We exchanged numbers and, months later, started dating. Here it was almost 2 years later, and he and I still hadn't had sex. It was now December 2002, and I was ready; he told me that he would wait on me to be ready and I finally was. One night that winter month, we had sex with protection. Days later, I get a phone call at 4AM from a young lady, asking me if he and I were still dating because I needed to know that she was 6 months pregnant from him.

Well, let's just say that, at times, I wish I had never met my oldest daughter's father. After having sex with him and assuming that I was the only woman he was seeing, I soon found that to be completely false. In fact, not only was he cheating, but he had gotten someone pregnant. This entire situation was unknown to me until after I decided to give myself to him. I immediately confronted him about his cheating and he confessed, but he also told me that I was pregnant. I asked him how he figured that, and he said it was because he had put holes in the condom and it broke.

I wanted to believe that a man I loved wouldn't do something like that. By then, I had begun working at a Krystal's Restaurant not far from my house. While working there I got really close to a few of my co-workers. I can remember it like it was yesterday: I was doing my job as usual and, all of a sudden, I ran to the bathroom and was vomiting all over the place. I came out and my friend said, "Renee you're pregnant", and I was like, "What do you mean, I *can't* be pregnant." I just knew that there was no way that I could have been pregnant because, when we had sex that night, he wore a condom and it never broke. I didn't know that he had put holes in the condom so that, when he was ready to ejaculate, I would be the recipient of his little swimmers. After taking a pregnancy test and receiving a plus sign, it was confirmed. I was pregnant.

How would I tell my parents that I was pregnant? This bothered me for a few days, and eventually, with the help of that same friend, I told them. They weren't upset because I had finished school and was working and wasn't an irresponsible child. I, however, felt guilty, as if I had let them down. Although I never once considered abortion, I was afraid to be a mother to someone.

I knew that my relationship was over with that cheating sperm donor but, for this child growing inside of me, I had to remain friendly. Throughout the entire pregnancy, he would come by off and on and visit me. Trying each time to reconcile and make things right. I declined. I just wanted him to do what was right by his child and support and take care of her. We made a verbal agreement that he would give me so much a month for his child, and we decided on a date that he would start. Let's just say that date came and went. So, I did what every mother who doesn't get any support does: I filled out the papers to put him on Child Support through the Department of Revenue.

Now, while I was pregnant--- more specifically September 13th 2003, which was 2 days before I gave birth to my girl--- I met the most handsome man I had laid eyes on in a long time. It's funny because he and I once sat down and talked about that first time we met--- he saw me and didn't know I was pregnant until I turned around. He said that from behind you could have never guessed.

He and I never exchanged numbers, but every time he came into town to visit his mom, we would meet up and visit or speak. I just never imagined that he would be the reason for me telling my story right now.

Diabetes is something that not a lot of people have tons of knowledge on. So, to complicate things, there is also what's called Gestational Diabetes. This is having diabetes while you're pregnant. Not a lot of mothers continue to have it after childbirth, but while pregnant it can be a living nightmare. I didn't find out until a month before I was scheduled to give birth that I was diabetic while pregnant. I ended up triggering it myself by drinking too much hot chocolate with sugar. I was sick, and that was the only thing that made me feel better. I ended up being insulin dependent until after I gave birth and, because I was diabetic, I risked a chance of having a baby being born over 10 pounds. Me' Kayla was due Sept 30$^{th}$ 2003 but, because on September 15$^{th}$ 2003 she was already almost 8 pounds and her lungs were fully developed (which was confirmed by amniocentesis), the decision was made to admit me and break my water. I was told that if I waited until Sept 30$^{th}$ my baby would be huge. Babies gain about 1.5-2 pounds a week in the last month.

After 9 hours of labor, she was born at 10:24 P.M. September 15, 2003, weighing 7 pounds and 13 ounces. Now that I was a mother and single, I knew that it was time to get things in motion and do what needed to be done for my child and me. Next stop was Advanced Career Training for Medical Assistance School.

I was in school just as long as I was pregnant the year before, 9 months. I learned how to draw blood, give injections, take vitals, run tests such as EGKs, and lots more. I graduated and finished my externship with Dr. Charles Simmons and his pediatric office on September 14, 2004. I immediately began searching for a job. It took me 3 months but, right before Christmas, I got hired by Solantic Urgent Care as a back office Medical Assistant.

Working for Solantic was a somewhat mixed experience. I loved the job, but I didn't like how they didn't like all the knowledge I had learned from school. So, after 3 months, I departed from them, moved on, and got a job with a family practice. That move was another challenge because now I was surrounded by a lot of females with a lot of drama. They argued or fussed about something almost daily. The staff was mixed races, but the office was much divided. I always got into it with this one chick in clerk and she always wanted to brush her mid-back-length hair. I got so angry one day that, when I was leaving work, I looked at her and pointed and said, "You have messed with me for the last time!" Everyone in the office was afraid of me the next day and thought that I had put some kind of root on the poor girl. When next she walked into the building, her long brunette hair she loved to brush was now shoulder length; she said that she went to the salon and was told her ends were extremely spit. Needless to say, I had nothing to do with that....or did I?

Months before I started working at Solantic Urgent Care, and on my cousin's birthday to be exact, I met someone who to this day is a part of me regardless of the situation. From the first day I met CT, we became inseparable. I was in love with him; he was a few years younger than me but I didn't care. We had sex often, and it just so happens one of those times I became pregnant. I actually found the ultrasound picture of the baby when I was packing my stuff up to move to Orlando. I got teary-eyed and had to put it back in the folder. I found out I was pregnant December 2005, but I never got to know the sex of the baby or hold the baby or anything. I went to the doctor and he told me that the baby had some severe swelling from the head down its back to its hind. The baby had Cystic Fibrosis which is VERY rare in African American babies. However, I didn't think it to be too rare; I knew that I had some Caucasian ancestors, so it would be possible. I was given two options: either wait to have a miscarriage or terminate the pregnancy. I had never experienced either one and, after talking to CT, his mom, my parents and a few others, I decided that terminating was the best option. I hated doing that so much. I cried for days. I was almost at the cutoff date for being able to terminate, so I could feel the baby moving and everything. I'd never wish that feeling on anyone, ever. To this day, I feel that my son or daughter is my guardian angel and is watching over me. CT and I remain friends, and he will tell anyone, even though he has a child now, that I had his first child.

There I was, twenty-three years old and feeling like I'd done everything a young adult should have done by this age. I was ready to meet someone who was going to love me and marry me. I had this three year old daughter from a sperm donor who did nothing for her, and I wanted more for her. I wanted someone who was going to love her as his own. I didn't know that I had met him September 13, 2003.

Sure I had met quite a few men from the time I graduated high school until then, but none of them stood out like he did. I was usually a sucker for light-skinned, clean cut men, but here he was, this brown-skinned, curly haired brother. He was standing in his mom's kitchen helping to prepare the meat for grilling. It was already past Labor Day weekend, but who cares, we were celebrating it regardless. I proceeded to the sitting area and grabbed a seat because I was already 9 months pregnant and due September 30, 2003. Because I was sitting, he never noticed that I was pregnant, or if I was standing he only saw me from behind. I did not look pregnant from behind at all. I noticed him noticing me watching him. He had come into town from Spartanburg, SC where he had been living for some time now. Was he alone? Of course he wasn't alone. He had brought with him a girlfriend and his two children.

What's that old saying, "You can look but don't touch"? That's just what I did. I knew he was taken, but I couldn't take my eyes off of him and I know the feeling was mutual. From that first time seeing him and every time he came in town after that I saw him. We talked and we were so close. People thought that I was his girlfriend, not knowing that whatever female came with him that trip was his girl. I didn't care because we had this bond that was unexplainable.

It was 2006, and his mom had gotten married the year before; I believe and she wanted to have something at her house to celebrate her wedding, since she had done the ceremony in Las Vegas. As always, it was a party to remember. We had all kinds of food, and my favorite: snow crab legs. Here was another event that I would get to see my friend. He brought with him yet another new girlfriend; this was like the third or fourth one since I had met him. I didn't care, because I knew that if he were mine he wouldn't want anyone else.

His kids were older, and his sister was even there so I got to meet her for the first time. We hit it off great, and had fun talking about the kids and just mingling. When you looked up he and I were together. Whether it was putting the crabs in the pot or standing by the tent talking, we were together. Finally, I felt it was time to just come out and let this man know that all of these years of wanting him had come to this moment. I didn't care that she had come there with him and neither did he. As a matter of fact, she ended up going in the bathroom and crying because he left to go to the store and she couldn't find him. She was a nice woman but definitely not his type. I was his type. Always had been his type. It was just never the right time until now.

I saw him sitting in the dining room and there were no empty seats so I walked up to him and sat down right next to him in the same seat. I whispered for him to give me his cell phone and I put my number in it. I then put his phone number in my cell and we continued to laugh and joke the rest of the night. This was in July of 2006. I gave him about a week and I picked up my phone and I called him. I didn't know where he worked or what time he went to work. I had called while he was just getting to work and he said he would call me as soon as he went on a break, and from that day on we talked on the phone every single day.

His birthday was coming up on August 28 and he didn't have any plans. By then we had started dating officially, so he said he would come and see me for the weekend of his birthday. Immediately I began planning our weekend. I was excited--- all the years of loving this man and waiting for the day was over. He was mine and I was his. I was on top of the world.

For his birthday weekend we went down to the river walk, we went to the beach, and we had some alone time as well. In preparation of his birthday, I had gone out to the mall and found this store, Frederick's of Hollywood, and saw this black lace halter night gown that stopped just above the knee and came with a black silk robe; I bought it for our special night. The first time I would ever do more than just be in his presence. That night, while he went to take his shower, I hurried and changed out of my clothes and put on this gown, and when he came out of the bathroom his mouth hit the floor. I had never done this for anyone ever, and I was nervous and so was he. I put on some music and I started dancing. First time I danced for a man. It all just came so natural and before I knew it he lifted me up in his arms, and because of his kissing me and caressing me and I was instantly relaxed. That night we made love, and I knew that this was the man that I wanted to marry.

Over the next few months we talked off and on about our past, present, and future and we talked about marriage and having a family together. Without any proposal, we came to the conclusion that we were going to become engaged to be married. We made a decision together, but were we rushing it? Yes, I'm sure now that it was rushed. But at that moment everything felt so right with us. It was like all my dreams were coming true. I could see myself plain and clear; as a child my best friend and I would sit in church and on the church program we would plan our dream weddings in that very church we sat in.

If I was going to marry this man I had to know it was right, so what better thing to do that than to move where he was and live with him as one. Sometimes things are better off left the way they are, because you just never know who someone really is until you're with them every day. This is what I discovered that next year.

## MAKING MARRIED MOVES

Spartanburg, South Carolina? Yes, that's where I moved to, December 2006. I was very excited, although some people saw my move as a waste of time and not a good decision. I didn't care. I was in love, engaged, and ready to start my life with the man of my dreams. He was already established and worked for a huge manufacturing company a few cities over. I immediately enrolled in school at the University of South Carolina Upstate and even got hired at Home Depot as a cashier. He told me I didn't have to work, just focus on school. But I'm as stubborn, as most Taurus women and men are, and I got a job anyway.

I began working and school had also started, so I was juggling both tasks. That semester I was doing very well in all of my classes and learning a lot at work. Just before my 90-day evaluation, a few co-workers that started with me and I were surprisingly terminated; all for various reasons, but all at the same time. We later learned that this company didn't like to pay their employees benefits unless they had been with the company already a good amount of years. So, the day after my birthday of 2007, I was jobless.

The summer was approaching and I was making sure all the wedding planning was in order. I never knew that people spent so much money and had to do so much stuff in making sure their day was just how they wanted it. My wedding dress went from just costing $400 to maxing out at like $1,000 after the accessories and all that went with it. I was also doing a lot of traveling back and forth monthly from Spartanburg to Jacksonville to see my daughter and to handle all the plans. By the time the last week of July came I was ready. August 4, 2007 was the coming Saturday and everything was paid for and arranged.

I had the biggest butterflies in my stomach as I stood there watching everyone in the wedding party walk down the aisles. I had chosen my cousin's song that she had with her group Pure Soul as the song for them to walk in on "We Must Be In Love". That's exactly what I felt: that we were in love and this was something that we were doing to make our love last a lifetime. After the song ended, Johnny Gill started singing "You For Me". I chose this song because, after hearing it in that Tyler Perry movie, I just knew this was the perfect song to walk down the aisle on. I know most people do the traditional "Here Comes the Bride" song but I had to be different. Why not? After all it was my special day.

Halfway down the aisle I got teary-eyed and started crying. I was about to marry the man that I was in love with from day one of meeting him that September day in 2003. I looked up at him the closer I got and he too was tearing up, and that didn't help me any. On that day August 4, 2007 I became Mrs. Renee' Burgess-Martinez. The decision to keep my surname was because of my oldest daughter having the last name Burgess and I felt more comfortable that way. From our wedding day until November things were fairly normal until one day, more specifically, the day that my monthly cycle was scheduled to start and it didn't. I went and bought a pregnancy test and it was negative so I figured maybe it's just late.

Two days later and still a no-show, so I went and got another test and it said I was pregnant! I was super excited and so ready for the new addition to our family. I immediately called and got an appointment with an OB/GYN. When the first appointment came all they did was some blood work and got some medical history and background information from the two of us.

The week of Thanksgiving that year of 2007 I became extremely sick and very nauseous, not keeping anything down, and I ended up dehydrated. I was asked to come to the doctor's office on November 21, 2007 and that morning I did; they gave me IV fluids and some nausea medicine to help me. While waiting for the fluids to run through the IV into my body, the doctor came into the room and asked him to step out of the room and he did.

Never in my life has anything ever seemed to go in slow motion like it did that day from that very moment after he walked out of the room. The doctor informed me that she had received my pre-natal labs and that everything was fine except one thing. My curiosity was small when she said that because I figured she saw that I had issues with diabetes while pregnant and that was the problem. Boy was I so wrong! She began to explain each lab and the results and then said that my blood work came back showing that I was HIV Positive. All I could do was stare at the freshly tan painted wall that had this one black smear on it where someone had put the back of the recliner chair on it and it left a scuff mark. I could not believe what I was hearing. Was I dreaming? Because if I was I wanted to wake up, quick! I wasn't dreaming: this was real, and her next words to me after I sat in silence for almost 5 minutes were "Do you want me to bring your husband back in?" My response was, "Yes, Bring him back in because if you're telling me I have this then he's the reason why!" She brought him back and I let her tell him while I looked at the expressions on his face. They weren't as if he was shocked at all. It was as if he said to himself, "Damn, she found out!" …You're damned right I "found out", and I was pissed to the highest level.

We left the doctor's office that moment and got into the car. We sat in silence for about 2 minutes and then he said to me of all things "Don't tell anyone; we will get through it ourselves". What in the fuck do you mean don't tell anyone? How could I go back to my house where my mom, daughter and aunt were visiting us for Thanksgiving and not say anything? I decided to just go in and go straight to my bed and lie down and not be bothered with anyone.

For almost 2 whole weeks I kept it to myself and the only other person who knew was the doctor's office. By then I had been back and found out that not only was I pregnant, but it was twins. Being such a high risk pregnancy, I was immediately placed on bed-rest and was only allowed to go out if it was somewhere I absolutely had to go. I had to quit my job that I loved so much.

One night, while driving to work before I was forced to quit, I had a break down. I was crying so hard that I couldn't even see the road in front of me and, to make matters worse, it was raining. As I finally got to my job and sat in the car before going in I did one of the hardest things I think I've EVER had to do. I called my mom the only person I knew I could talk to and she would know what to say to make me feel better. She answered the phone and I was crying so hard she thought something had happened to me. Once I got myself together, I began to make her remember how I was acting when she came to visit for Thanksgiving. Then I proceeded to tell her that I was acting so down and secluded because I had found out at the doctor that I was HIV positive and that my husband had infected me.

For the first time in a long time my mom didn't know what to say to me to make me feel better. In turn she began to cry and cry and cry. I didn't know if telling her was the right thing to do. Either way it was too late to take it back, it was now out there to her. She wanted to know what I was going to do. Was I going to stay? Was I going to leave? By then it was December 2007 so I decided to pack enough things for the month and drive to Jacksonville, FL and spend that time there with my family. I had forgotten that I purchased his sister and her kids' plane tickets to come and spend Christmas with us, but by that time I didn't even care. I just wanted to be left alone.

Before I left I got a call from a lady at the Spartanburg County Health Department and she asked me to come in to the office. This was routine for anyone who becomes infected. I went to her office and she began to ask me all these questions about my sexual history, my husband, and my pregnancy. I answered them but--- after answering all these questions, showing her how angry I was with my husband for doing this to me and giving her the names of women he had possibly been sleeping with--- she told me something that I will never forget. She said, “You should stay with your husband. You just got married and you’re pregnant. You don’t want to raise these kids by yourself.” I looked at her for a moment. This must be a woman who thinks that all men are perfect and that if she had a man and he had done this to her she would stay with him. I politely told her that I was not staying and would NEVER stay with someone who purposely lied, cheated, abused and hurt me mentally, physically and emotionally. She gave me a bag of condoms and sent me on my way.

I got home and, in a fury, I threw the bag at my husband and told him that if we EVER had sex again that he would be using the condoms. He said that I was his wife and no married couple uses condoms and he wasn’t using them. So I informed him that we would never be having sex again. He was lying in bed and turned over with his back to me while I stood on my side of the bed. All I heard was, “Whatever”. He was off work that night, which I hated because I just didn’t want to be around him. I was tired from throwing up so much with the nausea and vomiting still bothering me. So I went to bed and I can remember this so vividly: ladies you know how your man tries to sneak and wake you up in the middle of the night with a little poke? Well I could feel him touching me but I was so tired that I didn't realize that he was turning me over on my back. He took everything I had on off. Next thing I know, this man climbed on top of me and started having sex with me. I woke up and tried to move him but I was so weak. He leaned down and said in my ear, "You're my wife and I will have sex with you whenever I want and how I want!" After struggling to get him off of me and losing I started to cry. Tears rolled down my face to my pillow. I must have blacked out because when I woke up I was in the bathroom in a tub of water with the door locked. He was knocking on the door asking me if I was ok. I didn't respond. All I could gather was that, when I finally was able to get up, I ran myself a bath and fell asleep in there. The water by then was almost chilly. After realizing what just happened to me and that I was just literally raped by my husband, I knew without a doubt I had to get away as soon as I could.

During my time away, I went through a series of emotions that varied from sadness to rage. However, I managed to pull myself together enough to go back to my home in Spartanburg with one intention: to get every last thing that I owned. I went back December 27, 2007 the day before his sister was scheduled to fly out and go back to New York. Once she left, I noticed that there were a few things that needed to be picked up from the store. So we were riding in the car on our way to the store and I just burst out laughing. He asks me what was so funny and looked around because I have a tendency to always see the funniest things while driving. Not this time. What I said out of my mouth next let me know that it was time for me to leave. I said, "Oh, I just thought of a new way to kill you today!" I've seen plenty of horror movies, and I know that look of fear on a person's face when they are in total shock and are scared to the bone. From that moment until I left he was completely afraid of me to the point that he wouldn't sleep in the room with me. His bed was now the couch, and if I made a move in the middle of the night he woke up, making sure that it wasn't a move to try what I was longing to do to him. Never in my life had I ever had a thought to kill anyone but, with his infecting me and putting two unborn lives at risk without thinking, I would have done it. But that was just it: I was pregnant. And I thought about how I would probably be in jail for murder and give birth to kids that I'd never get to see. So I did what was right, and I left the situation that was causing me so much pain.

It was New Years Day and I was in a great mood and so was he, although it was for different reasons. My happiness was that of feeling able and ready to let go and move on. His happiness was because we had a talk about how disappointed I was with him and how I would never forget what he did to me, but would be able to eventually forgive him. I guess he took that as me saying I wasn't going to leave him; little did he know I was planning on that very day to pack every single thing I came into that marriage with and leaving.

As the time approached for him to leave for work, I was already thinking what I had to do when he stepped foot out of that door. I picked up the phone and I called my very close and dear friend, and I also called my cousin whom I had only just met since moving to Spartanburg. He and I are 8 years apart, so by the time his parents weren't together anymore I wasn't even born yet. Any who, I told them both of the entire situation leading up to that point, and I asked if they could please come and help me move my stuff out of my apartment. Had I been really thinking, I would have tossed all his little bit of shit out to the dumpster. I didn't though, and I in turn removed myself from the situation.

We took from about 8 pm that evening until about 4 or 5 am to get everything that was mine out. What I didn't pack inside my truck to take back to Jacksonville, FL with me I left at my friends house to come and get at a later date.

Now here it is the next morning, January 2, 2008, and he's finally off of work. I can imagine when he walks in the door and notices things missing here and there and goes into the bedroom and see's all his clothes on the floor and the bed is gone he's going to flip out. Sike! This unmoved man calls my phone and, after about 3 to 4 times, I finally answer. Do you know what he says to me? "Why didn't you leave me something to cook in the oven with?" My response was simply, "I left you with exactly what you had when I came!" and I hung up the phone. He thought I had already left and gone back to Jacksonville but I was in Boiling Springs, SC at my friend house sleeping on her sofa until I was rested enough to drive to Florida.

I cried my entire drive of 5 hours and some minutes back to the place where I should have never left. Gospel music was the only thing I wanted to hear and then it began to play with my emotions. I understood that what was done to me was completely wrong and then I wondered--- well--- how God could allow this to happen to me. I wasn't promiscuous at all and I could count on one hand the amount of men I had ever slept with in my entire life. I just couldn't understand why. Always knew that it was never my place to question God's reasons for things, but all that was out the window; I wanted answers. Later on I discovered the answers I was seeking.

Never did I think that the next chapter of my life was going to be the hardest to deal with on every level possible. I still to this day have no idea where I got the strength from, but I did it.

## HOMECOMING "COURT"

Welcome to Florida, the Sunshine State! It had been a year since I had moved away and here I was moving back home to my parents house. Nobody ever expects to get married and separate so fast. As I drove across the state line I almost felt like I wanted to turn back around and go back to my husband. Don't get me wrong, infecting me and not telling me up front about his status was completely wrong and absolutely devastating. But I was in love with this man. When I first met him it was a love at first sight moment and all, so I knew I would have to use my strength and not allow myself to overlook the loss of trust I had in him. I held my head high and I pulled into my parents' driveway, got out the car, was met by my mother and we shared the longest hug we had ever had in my entire 24 years of life.

I've never been really affectionate with my parents at all. I hated hugs and kisses. So to get the love I was receiving from them brought out some new responses on my part that I never knew I had. Ok, well I had them for the men in my life....There I said it! But there's nothing like the love from your parents.

The month of January proved to be the beginning of the longest year ever. I have never been one to snoop and search for information unless I'm given a reason to not trust what I'm being told. Something told me to start checking things because I had found out from my husband's sister that, while I was gone the entire month of December, a woman and my husband were new parents to a baby girl. Shocked? Hell Yes! What do you mean he has a child with someone else and we are married? Well this information unfolded when I called my husband's sister to tell her why I wasn't there when she first flew in to SC for Christmas. Upon telling her that her brother had knowingly infected me with HIV, she was in disbelief because she didn't even know about his status. She was silent for a few minutes and then she finally came out and said, "Well, Renee', while I was there visiting he took me to a woman's house and told me, 'Look at the baby, doesn't she look just like me?'" His sister in return asked him, “What do you mean look like you? Is this your child?” To her surprise he said, “Yes.” The next thing she wanted to know from him was did I know about the woman or the child. Do you know this motherfucker had the nerve to say that I knew and that I was ok with it? What was even worse than that was that he told this woman and many other people that I wasn’t his wife, but I was just living with him and was his roommate. It bothered me. However, being that I was about to move on from him, I didn’t let it bother me as badly as it could have.

I hung up with her in such anger that I called him and asked him, and he told me that his sister was lying and that the baby was not his, but the baby of a friend with whom he worked. I then remembered the incident when I first moved to SC and a woman came bringing him a Christmas gift. I knew right then I was dealing not only with a cheater, but with a pathological liar. What I did next shocked everyone and stirred up the entire state of South Carolina.

We shared a joint cell phone account and, although we didn’t receive detailed invoices in mail, I could log in online and see all the calls made and calls received. I took a deep breath and I dialed every single number that I didn’t know. I spoke with women who were friends but had slept with him in the past. I talked to women who said they were supposed to be his girlfriend at that moment. Hell, I even talked to a MAN who said, "Yea I know him, what you mean you're his wife? He told me that he only liked men and that I was his one and only!" I laughed at that one. In end, that had to be almost 150-200 calls that were made during the entire time we had the joint phones. I proceeded to inform them that he was HIV positive and that, if they in fact slept with him, then they needed to go and get tested. Some cursed me out, some thanked me, and some just hang the phone up. I didn't care I did my job.

It took everything I had in me to not get in my car and drive back to Spartanburg and kill this man. I had wanted to kill him before, but this time I was at an all-time high of rage. After I calmed down--- because keep in mind I'm still pregnant and not due to deliver until July 13, 2008--- I decided to cut myself off from him for a little bit. I ignored his calls and texts of him wanting me to come back home and make things work.

Later that month I got a call from my aunt rushing me to turn the TV on to the news. There had been a case of a homosexual couple where the older man knowingly infected the younger man and was sentenced to 5 years in prison with the felony crime of knowingly infecting others with HIV. I knew that very moment that what was done to me, as his wife or not, was a crime. And I wanted nothing but for him to be punished. After thinking things through and making sure that was what I wanted to do, I picked up the phone and called the Jacksonville Sheriff's Office and was put in contact with a detective in the sex crimes unit. He informed me of the steps that needed to be taken, and the first thing was to file a police report. I didn't want to file a report with just any officer, so I contacted an officer who I had known for year s and he came over and took the report for me. Once it was filed, they had gathered all information they needed.

Here it was now, February 14, 2008, Valentine's Day. The phone rings and it's the detective letting me know that everything was gathered, but they just needed one last piece of evidence to stick, and that involved a recorded confession. He told me all the questions that they needed answers to and asked me if I could do a three-way conversation with my husband to record the answers. I asked him to give me a few minutes to make sure I knew how to approach this and to also make sure he was awake and able to talk to me. About 20 minutes passed and the detective called me back and I was ready. He had no idea how I was about to get the answer that we all basically wanted to know. The phone rings and he answers as if he was expecting me to call back. He says, "I want you to come back home, we can work this out." That gave me the chance to begin my purpose for calling. I said to him, "Well, I have to go see a psychologist and, on my first visit, they gave me a list of questions and, in order for me to get the treatment they want to give to help me heal mentally, I got to know this information from you." He asked me to read the questions, so I went down my list of nine to ten and he answered every single question. They ranged from when he knew he was infected to why he didn't tell me. These are questions I had asked him for months but could never get a reply to. All of a sudden, because he wants me to come home, he's singing like a canary bird. I ended the conversation immediately after that with a quick, "I love you," and when I clicked him off the line I said to the detective, "YOU GOT IT?!" He said, "Yes I got it!" A few days later I was informed that they had the grounds to issue a nationwide warrant for his arrest and that once they got him in custody they would be working on extraditing him back to Florida to faces his charges.

While I was waiting to hear back from the detective, on the morning of March 22, 2008 I woke up about 9 am and realized that I was lying in wet sheets. Moving my covers I realized that possibly my water had broken. I had never experienced this before because with my oldest daughter they broke my water. I remembered that if I put on a sanitary pad and in a few minutes it soaked that my water was indeed broken. I immediately called my parents who had stepped out to grocery shop and, once they rushed back, I rushed to the Shands Jacksonville Pregnancy Emergency Room. Once there I was hooked up to all these monitors and IV fluids. I ended up having to get a catheter and after hours of waiting to see what they wanted to do the decision was made to do an emergency cesarean section and get the babies out.

I was given local anesthetics and felt not one thing from my waist down. It was now about 8:15 PM and they started with the first incision; out first was Michelle. They quickly brought her to me so see and then took her away. She was making sounds so that made my scared little heart feel a bit better. Next out was Micah, and I quickly looked at him and he was taken away also. So tiny they could fit in the palms of my hands. Micah was born weighing 1 pound and 7 ounces and Michelle weighed 1 pound and 6 ounces.

It wasn't anything new to me to have no father of my child, or in this case, children, being in the room. With my oldest daughter's father he wasn't there so this time my mom didn't come in the room. But Miss Pam was there; she was our neighbor across the street and a very good friend to me. She had been there at every single doctor's appointment and she was going to do the baby shower like she had done for my oldest. Except this time the baby shower would have to come after the babies were already here.

Michelle and Micah were placed on what seemed to be thousands of tubes and wires. They both had to have ventilators to help them breathe and everything. The first time I saw them I was so scared and I wanted to cry but I couldn't, God wouldn't allow me to cry at all. I knew the moment that I looked into their eyes I had to be one of the strongest people in their lives. They needed me as much as I needed them. I thought about the time I wanted to kill myself and how if I had done that I would have taken two innocent lives with me.

While in the hospital in the NICU both twins endured surgery, with Micah to this day still having surgeries. He is my fighter and for 5 years now he has proven all of the doctors wrong. I remember when Micah was in the NICU there was a doctor who had come over from St. Vincent's to help the Neuro team at Shands NICU. When Micah was 3 weeks old he started having seizures that resulted in the hydrocephalus and the Grade 4 IVH bleeding on the brain. She told me that I should pull the plug on him and that he would be a vegetable his entire life. I almost punched this doctor but God intervened and I told the doctor that she was wrong and MY GOD! She was 10000000% wrong. My son does things you wouldn't think a child who they claim only has 10% of his brain tissue left could do. You read right, 10% brain tissue. If that's not a miracle then I don't know what is. My son laughs, claps, kicks his little legs, eats by mouth, loves drinking water from a cup, plays with toys, and most of all HE IS ALIVE!

During this time I knew there was no way possible that I could ever date again but I ended up meeting someone through mutual friends. Come to find out our parents were High School classmates. We were both into music. He could produce the hell out of some music and I was doing my radio show. He introduced me to a lot of things. One being that the fear I had of having sex again didn't have to be. People assumed that because we were always together that we were either in a relationship or having sex. We were having sex. The last time I had sex was with my husband and it was the time when he forced himself on me. I was completely afraid that the next time I had sex that I would cry and unless he's reading this book he'll never know that I did cry. Tears rolled down my eyes and all I could think about was that moment that made me feel so disgusting. When he finally lifted his head from my neck and looked me in my eyes and I saw it was him and not my husband I snapped out of it and came back to reality. It was almost if I was a virgin all over again and that was my first time having sex. Technically I was a virgin. I was a newly infected person with HIV having sex for the first time. For those inquiring minds, yes I did tell him my status before we ever had sex. We were friends before we were ever sexual partners. That lasted until he moved and relocated to another city and state. To this day I miss him but we are still the very best of friends.

Now here is it end of April early May of 2008. And--- if I might say--- my ex husband is such a momma's boy, being that he is her only child. When he was arrested the first time she bailed him out, and again the second time. However, that third time there was no bailing him out. Now the second time he was placed on house arrest and only allowed to go to the doctor, church, and the grocery store. Also during that second time, the state of South Carolina got wind of what he had done and, by us living in their state; they were also able to file charges. That became tricky because when it comes to the law no one person is able to be charged with the same crime for the same person twice. So it was down to which state was going to move first. The penalty for this felony crime in South Carolina was 10 years plus a $5,000 fine; in Florida the penalty was 5 years. I received a call from the detective informing me that he was in the process of being extradited to the state of Florida and would be placed in jail without bond until the hearing.

Here it is now, September 17, 2008, and I was told that I had to appear in court for his sentencing hearing. Before the court was brought in session the judge went into his chambers to listen to the recording of his confession. Then, he came out. The look on his face was scary. This judge had noticeable anger in his face and he asked me to stand in front of the court and speak. The state Attorney representing had already told me to prepare something to say to the courts and to him. The date on the letter what the date that I wrote this:

August 16, 2008

To Whom It May Concern:

Your Honor,

I am writing you this letter to express to you how my life has changed since I found out about my HIV status the day before Thanksgiving. It is so hard to write this letter to you because I'm still in a healing process. I'm sure by the end of this letter I will be in tears. I have gone through emotional changes that have led me to be at one point depressed and even suicidal. I have to suffer financially because when I left South Carolina and returned here to Florida I had to withdraw from school and because I was receiving financial aid I am forced to pay back the Dept. of Education. I'm in debt with the apartment I was living in located in South Carolina. I have to seek counseling and learn to readjust my life in society. I am in constant fear that everyone is watching me and that they know I have HIV.

I try to use my experience as an eye opener and do motivational speaking to men and women of all races to become aware and know their partner's status. No matter how strong I try to be my mind will never let me forget. I close my eyes and I see him and I hear the words he told me sitting in my car when we walked out the doctor's office after I found out and that was "Don't tell anyone". How could I not tell anyone about something that could kill me one day and take me from the ones who love me and they not know why? What's even more painful and hurtful is that I had to learn that I was not his only victim and that my children were not his only newborn infants exposed. There are other victims in South Carolina and to my knowledge one other person has come forward with charges. I felt as a person who respects the law it was my duty to do what was right and file a report. How could I let this man remain free in the world knowing what he has done to me he could do to the next person. I loved my husband but all it took was for him to open his mouth and say a few sentences to let me know his status. I asked on numerous occasions before we ever had sex and absolutely before we got married and was told he was fine and there was nothing to worry about. Like I told him upon finding out he would have never know what I would have done. I am a medical assistant so I if I decided to be with him I would have said ok let's find out what we can do to protect ME. He didn't take that into consideration at all he planned to do me like all those before me and say nothing. God blessed me with 2 beautiful babies who if not had been conceived would have not revealed the truth. If I had not had those prenatal labs when I did, I would not have known until my next yearly physical that he had given me this horrible and deadly disease. Not only has he done this to me but also my twins had the possibility of being exposed and I praise God everyday for their current negative status. They do however have to be tested throughout their life. I gave birth to our twins Michelle and Micah Martinez on March 22, 2008. They were born at 23 weeks and 6 days gestation, which is only 1 day from being 6 months pregnant. My son Micah was born 1 pound and 7 ounces and is almost 4 months and is still in the Neonatal Intensive Care Unit. He had a massive bleed to the brain in all ventricles and now had hydrocephalus, which is fluid on the brain. Since birth he has had to have 9 surgeries. Michelle was born 1 pound and 6 ounces, had a small bleed on her brain, 1 surgery and a total of 2 chest tubes. She was discharged on June 24th and was sent home on oxygen and a heart monitor. Both babies are on disability and have extreme special needs and will always have to be handled with extra precautions.

My family has been torn by this whole situation. My mom had a Sickle Cell Anemia Crisis when I told her my status. My father suffers high blood pressure and when he found out he had a serious hypertension episode. I have lost the love of his family members that I truly cared about especially his mom. Even though she knew I can in no way hold her responsible for his actions. I was upset for her knowing and not saying anything but overall it was his obligation to tell me. My parents have also gone into debt because they spent thousands of dollars for our wedding because they wanted me, their only daughter, to have the wedding of my dreams. I was only married to him 3 months before finding out I had HIV and after leaving in January 2008 I found out that he had cheated and had affairs with many other women and possibly men. His cheating was no gossip topic; I spoke directly to two of the women who were involved with him while we were together.

My life will never be the same again and I will forever have this. I struggle everyday to take 3 medications. I have never in my 25 years of life had to take medicine on a regular basis and at this age I have to always. I know Florida offers the maximum of 5 years for this crime but I'm asking you to consider the fact that this is a lifetime death sentence he has placed on me. Yes I know that things are more advanced now and I can live longer but my life has been altered by his rage and vendetta. Everything I do I have to be cautious and careful, a mosquito bite, a scratch, anything that could expose anyone around me. I think a crime like this deserves punishment equal to what it causes long-term, lifetime pain, and that's way more than 5 years.

In closing my letter Your Honor I ask that you take into consideration when sentencing that what Gregory has given me is for a lifetime. I will never be able to work because I have to be the medical caregiver to my children. I will never have a regular relationship with anyone. I am obligated to reveal my status to anyone who I become involved in a relationship with and will face rejection I'm sure more than acceptance. I would not wish this on anyone and I pray that the justice system keeps this man, Gregory Sean Martinez, in jail for as long as they can to prevent his obvious trend of spreading one of the world's deadliest diseases.

Sincerely,

Renee' Yvette Burgess-Martinez

Wow, just going back through and reading this letter myself now in 2013 gives me chills. I can remember sitting down and writing this letter and crying the entire time. When I stood in front of the judge and court on September 17, 2008 I cried, and the tears were not of sadness but of pure hurt. I was hurting, and I still loved this man even as he stood there in chains. When you truly love someone it's hard to let them go from your heart, but I knew I had to.

So when the judge issued his official sentencing terms his mom, aunt, and I guess cousin and his wife were there sitting in front of us in the court. They blurted out that I was a liar and I was not telling the truth and blah, blah, blah. It was almost as if they didn't know they were at a sentencing hearing and that he had already plead guilty. Did their words bother me? NO! Hell No! If she wanted to spare her son from going to prison then she should have opened her mouth and told me. I know there's a lot that goes into disclosing the status of someone else, but it was her son that I married, and she should have made sure without trying to be subliminal about it or beating around the bush.

On that date, Gregory Sean Martinez was sentenced to 5 years in prison and given 6 months of time served. So that made his sentence 4 and a half years total.

The year of 2008 brought a lot of new changes in my life but, on a more positive side of things, I connected with a few people that helped me to be able to do what I love to do, and that's radio. I met Ablaze Da Architek and when I met him he had a website called Curb Nerds. It was a social networking site for musicians, artists, and just anyone who had a love for music. Once I saw the site and saw that Ablaze was trying to find a way to bring the music of artists on the site to a fan base of listeners, I threw out the idea of creating radio show. He asked me if I would host it and I accepted the challenge. Doing radio broadcasting is my life passion. Anyone who truly knows LadyByrd knows that I love it! So I went to a famous site for internet radio and I created a show and named it Curb Nerds

Radio. This was July 25, 2008 and we launched the very first LIVE show and to this date the first show has archived 295 listens, had 37 live listeners, and 16 live callers.

It was almost the end of the year and I had been back in Jacksonville for almost a year. And every time I went somewhere a man was approaching me for my phone number or just for conversation, and I would blow them off. Sure I'm not an ugly woman, but at that point I just started feeling pure ugly about myself. I didn't like the person I saw in the mirror. I felt like I was just awful. So it began……..

# TRIAL AND ERROR

The depression had begun and I didn't even know it. I was so into keeping myself busy that I just completely overlooked the idea. By May of 2009 I had found myself a job. I had tried to go back to school because here it was 7 years later and I still didn't have my Associates degree. That should have taken me 2 years or less to complete; however, I was determined to get it. So while working part time doing inventory, I was also taking classes at the community college to complete my degree.

Around the end of 2008 I decided to date again. For me I found it easier to date long distance, but this was a huge challenge. I had tried a few positive dating websites for those infected with HIV; this was a failure. Then I was introduced to this website called *I See Color*. It was a social networking site that was started by Michael Baisden; I registered to the site Dec 1, 2008 World AIDS Day and immediately started talking about my status on my page because, whether it was for friendship or more, I wanted this to be something known on my page up front. After a few months I befriended a guy on there and he inboxed me and disclosed that he too was HIV Positive. This made me smile because I felt that I was making progress towards happiness and away from depression. We exchanged numbers and, as time went on, we ended up in a long distance relationship.

Having a long distance relationship allowed me to be loved but from a distance. I still wasn't comfortable with a lot of things so to have someone love and care about me like he did felt good. Eventually, being that he lived in Oklahoma, things slowly went south. One reason was that he was still struggling with the acceptance of his HIV status and fell into a deep depression, which caused him to shut me out completely. I didn't pressure or push him to talk to me. I just moved on. A long time friend I had from being on Yahoo chat and I had been kind of off-and-on long distance relationship dating, and we found ourselves back on. We were so back on that not only did this man go and get my name tattooed on his arm, but he also mailed me an engagement ring in the mail. YEP! He mailed me a ring. I was totally shocked, and I just knew that he was serious about us being together. What other reason would I have to think otherwise? I had known him since about 2001-2002. Had never met him, but I trusted him. Come to find out he wasn't who I thought he was; he wanted me and his baby momma, and some other chick. I immediately ended that and moved on.

I met this guy who was in the Navy and had just been stationed in Jacksonville. Now keep in mind this was while I was yet trying to figure out how to disclose my status to men that I would potentially date who didn't already know me or about my status. At the time, I was saying to myself, "Ok, well, I will see if the guy is interested in having a full relationship with me first, and if so then I can tell him once I know." This guy and I had gone on about 3-4 dates, and he told me on that 4th date that he saw himself having a relationship with me and wanted to be my boyfriend. I then knew I HAD to disclose my status to him. Well when I told him, he cursed me out, kicked me out of his car on the other side of town where you have to cross the bridge, and left me stranded. Luckily for me I had friends over there, so I called one of them and they came and got me and took me home. I was living with my parents at the time, and they were so protective (and still are) of me that I just didn't say anything. So reading this book will be the first time they know of this. Yes, awkward moment for sure.

With all of this going on and trying to go to school, my son became sick, and I faced having to withdraw from my classes. There was just so much going on that I didn't know what to do.

I got to a point I can honestly say that I stopped taking my medicine and I stopped wanting to do a lot of things. I was giving up physically and mentally.

In 2009, I was presented with yet another huge decision, and that was did I want to divorce my husband and, if so, would it be while he was incarcerated or after he was released. I chose to do it while he was still in jail. Being that my income was limited, I was able to go through legal aid and file my papers and set up a payment plan that would allow me to pay monthly on the cost of divorce. As of August 2009 I was divorced to the man whom I had yearned at one point to spend the rest of my life with. It was no easy thing either. We had to do mediation and they allowed him to call into the mediation from jail. He wanted to ask for a paternity test. What the hell do you mean paternity? Are you out of your damn mind? That's what I wanted to know. Not only did both of my twins look just like him, but Michelle was the damn near spitting image of him and all of his biological children. There was no denying his children, not to mention I have never cheated on anyone in my life and definitely wouldn't cheat on my husband! I was completely appalled at his accusations. He was the one that was cheating.

Afterwards, I nevertheless moved forward, and here I was back in school to get this associates degree that I had been trying to get for so long. I was still working and, for the rest of 2009 going into 2010, I was focused on school and work. I was so comfortable with how things in my life were beginning to go, I decided that I would try dating again. I decided to join a dating website for positive individuals and I met this guy who I was immediately attracted to. Not only was he educated but also he was so damn handsome. Of course, he didn't live in Florida but in Missouri. We talked every single day and decided that we wanted to meet and we did. He came to FL and we spent time together on two different occasions. For whatever reasons we didn't work out and, after two months, that little fun journey was over, though we remained friends. I found out later the next year that he had gotten married and that hurt me but, like I always say, things happen on God's time and in his plans, so I just had to be happy for him.

Everyone knows that I am a Facebook junkie; I just might be the most addicted person to Facebook that you know. Well, I had added a friend who was a mutual friend with a few people on my page. We exchanged conversation from time to time and then one day we just had a very full conversation that included the exchange of phone numbers. He lived in South Carolina and he had a daughter that was close in age to my daughter so that worked out well. As time went on we found ourselves in a long distance relationship and decided around November of 2010 that, for Christmas, my mom, kids and I would take a trip with him and his daughter to North Carolina to his mom's house. What was so exciting about this was that I was meeting his family, but also that there was a chance that it was going to snow. We arrived there safely, and those days spent there were the best. We had some great food, great bonding, and some entertainment. Yes, entertainment. My mom is going to get me, but I don't care. Now, I know better than to wear socks in any house that has stairs. When I lived in my apartment in South Carolina with my ex-husband we had stairs, and I saw my life flash before my eyes a few times on the stairs we had. So I knew to be extra careful on stairs. All I know is she was holding my twin girl, and they were heading down stairs and bloop, bloop, bloop... By the time we all got to the stairs they were both down the stairs and, Lord, my being the tickle box I am, I hollered in laughter. My laughter made my mom laugh and think less about the pain she had just inflicted on her ass. Oh and guess what else! It snowed on Christmas day and my kids got to see snow for the very first time ever! My oldest was so excited; we made snowballs and had fights, we made snow angels and we made a snowman. Sad to say that the relationship ended, but we are also very good friends and he knows and I know that the love we had for each other is still there.

Now, as I stand in this line waiting, my feet start to hurt. But I had been waiting on this moment since I started in August of 2002, so there was no turning back now. It took me 8 years, but, as of August 27, 2010 I was not just Renee' Burgess-Martinez the mother, but I was Renee' Burgess-Martinez the college graduate with an Associates in Arts Degree from Florida State College of Jacksonville. What a long road and journey this was for me, but I did it and I was so excited! When I gave that lady my name card and I heard her call it out as I walked across the stage, all I wanted to do was jump up and down. I had accomplished quite a few things in life, but this was one that presented a challenge to me no matter how hard I had tried to finish.

I tell people all the time that when you least expect it God steps in, and He's always on time. I was at a point in my life that I had finally decided on what I wanted to do and the direction I wanted to go, but as time went on and even now I have learned that what you want and where you want to go and do isn't always up to you.

As the New Year came in, I was excited that I was able to start college and work toward my bachelor's degree at the University of North Florida. I was taking 5 classes 4 on campus and one online and I was so focused. Then--- you guessed it--- my son got sick and I ended up having to do a medical withdrawal from the school. I was very discouraged, but that didn't stop me and I didn't give up.

Although I wasn't working, I still made sure my kids were taken care of with help from my parents and the kids' Godparents, so things were ok. I was still missing that thing that made me feel amazing inside and that was the love of a man. Don't ask me why I felt that I needed to have a man to feel amazing, because if you asked me now I'd say I don't need man to be the amazing person I am today. However, back then I felt that it was all I wanted.

Since graduating, I was thinking of my next steps with my education, and I knew my passion was radio broadcasting but it was hard to find a college that offered that as a degree. In the midst of that, I found out that I had a love for something else: Speech Language Pathology. I went to the career center at the college and found 3 schools in the state of Florida that had that exact major, and with none being in Jacksonville I had to decide where to go. There was the University of Florida in Gainesville, and then you had Florida State University in Tallahassee, and the University of Central Florida in Orlando. Of the three schools only one had a continuous enrollment and you didn't have to apply to the program and hope you made the cut, and that was UCF in Orlando. So I applied to the school and, after getting them all the information they needed, I was accepted and began classes August of 2011.

I had to look at a lot of factors when choosing to go to this school. I would have to move and I had to figure out if I was going to move all the kids with me or just the twins or what. Being that my dad is a truck driver and gone most of the week and my mom doesn't really need to be left home alone, we sat down, talked, and decided that my girls would stay there with her while my son and I moved to Orlando for school. I found a school right next to the college that dealt with special needs children so I applied for him to go there and he was accepted. I then made sure I found an apartment, and I think I found the best apartments in Orlando. For a one bed, one bath, washer/dryer in apartment, water, sewer, and pest control included in the rent all for just over $650 a month. I found my son a special needs school that was literally on the campus of UCF, so everything was right there for me. I loved my classes and I enjoyed the feeling of being a student and actually experiencing what I considered real college life.

Upon moving I had already decided that I wanted to find a church that I would be comfortable going to and one that had a very nice family-oriented vibe. I searched and up popped Greater Macedonia Missionary Baptist Church, Inc. and that August I visit the church for the very first time. I can't explain the feeling that I felt when I walked into the church and was greeted by so many people who I didn't know, but who made me feel right at home. As service went on, they did the announcements and then asked all the visitors to stand so, as I stood listening to the other visitors give their greeting, it was finally my turn. I introduced myself, "I'm Renee Burgess-Martinez and this is my son Micah Martinez and we're from Jacksonville, Florida and I recently relocated here for school at the University of Central Florida." I was about to sit down then the pastor asked, "What's your major?" and with so much confidence I said, "Speech Language Pathology!" He said, "WELL ALRIGHT NOW!" and I sat down huge smile inside of course. Next thing that won me over was the sermon. The sermon was titled "Decisions,

Decisions, Decisions". Guess what? I had to make a few hard decisions when moving and I was a bit weary as to if I made the right choice, and that sermon confirmed that I was making the best choice possible. So to Pastor Willie C. Barnes, the pastor of this great church in historic Eatonville, Florida I thank you with my all! The almost 2 years I was blessed to sit in your congregation was amazing. I even got closely acquainted with a few of the members of the church and, although I was moved to actually join the church many times, I had a feeling my stay in Orlando was going to be short-lived.

While in Orlando I decided that I wanted to start dating again. Now this was a very hard decision for me because I had just gone through something I had never in my life had to deal with and that had been a stalker! It all began when I accepted a friend request on Facebook from a guy who had over 20 mutual friends with me. So I'm like ok his name looks familiar, and I didn't really deny anyone so I added him. Immediately he started liking every single thing on my page. Every post, every picture, everything he hit the like button. I figured that he was just checking out my page being that he was new to it. Not once did I think he was crazy. As days went on he started inbox messages with me and flirting. It was around December and days before Christmas. He posted on his page how is mom wasn't cooking and all he wanted was some collard greens and some cake. Me being that person that I am I told him my dad had just cooked a nice big pot of greens and if he wanted I could bring him some. He was happy and said yes. I got his address which was in Sherwood not far from my parents and I took it to him. Didn't even get out of the car I literally handed him the bag through the window.

Days went on and his contact with me grew. I ended up around that time having a hard time walking and was ill. I had got an ingrown hair on my inner thigh that I was forced to go to the ER and let them cut open and pack with sterile gauze. Let me tell you that was the worst pain I had experienced in a long time. Anyway, he started talking about dating and having a relationship and I just wasn't ready. This was also around the time when we were given links to the videos we did for *The Faces of HIV* exhibit. I posted my link on my FB page because, keep in mind, at this point only those close to me knew about my HIV status. It wasn't a secret, but you know people have so many things going on in their lives they don't pay attention to others lives. I immediately got lots of responses to my video posting. One response in particular by a woman named Risa stuck with me and became a motivator. She said this:

> "Renee, because of brave and selfless people like you, there will be greater awareness of this disease. HIV doesn't have a certain 'look'. You don't have to be an emaciated drug user, a promiscuous individual, or a homosexual to have this; this is everyone's disease, and we are all at risk. We all need to make the commitment to get tested, embrace monogamy, and educate our youth to do the same. HIV is not going away."

That immediately let me know that what I had begun on this journey with *The Faces of HIV Project* was going to be awesome.

So my status was not hidden to him at all. He was among the first to see my video. After multiple times of refusing to be in a relationship with this man, he proceeded to curse me out. He would call my phone so many times that nobody else could even get through to my phone and I could barely make a phone call. Keep in mind I was still living in Orlando and had gone back after Christmas. He found my address there and threatened to come there and kill me. He found my parents address and went there leaving a note saying to please ask me to call him.

Things got so bad I had to change my phone number and I had to call the police. They ended up warning him but that didn't help; he still found ways around that. He would find me on YouTube and on Twitter and leave messages and posts on my stuff. All of this because I told this man I didn't want to be with him. Oh and it got worse. He then proceeded to find an old video from a phone interview I did with a South Carolina News station and post it all over FB and telling people that he slept with me and that I infected him with HIV. First of all, I didn't sleep with this man and if I had it would have been protected. He made himself look like a complete fool with his comments and the video posting because I'm here in the video telling how I had my husband put in jail for infecting me; why would I turn around and do that to anyone else? Exactly… I wouldn't.  So after a while he got the picture and left me alone. This finally ceased by the end of January 2012.

Now that all that was over I could finally enjoy the year of 2012. I said "This is my year!"  I was so right about that! I found the place where "Black People Meet"!

UNEXPECTED HAPPINESS ENDING

**A little about me...**

I am a very goal-oriented individual who loves to have fun but knows when to be serious about life. I am 100% trustworthy and am an open book with nothing to hide. God is my daily strength in everything that I do, and He guides me through all my paths. I am currently in college pursuing a degree in Speech-Language Pathology. As you can tell I'm a very devoted Christian and I love God above all!

---

**About the one I'm looking for...**

I am looking for someone who is educated, understanding, compassionate, and who can bring to my life that one piece of joy I've been missing which is Love. I love shooting pool so he's got to be some great competition! Honesty is big with me and communication. If we can't communicate as mature adults then it's not a good fit at all.

**I'd just like to add…**

I am HIV Positive and I am VERY open about my status, as I am an activist for the cause as well as a motivational speaker. I was infected by my ex-husband, who is serving a jail sentence for the crime. So if my status is a problem for you, I apologize and I wish you well with your search to find Love. Sorry!

When you think about what you want to say about yourself on a dating website you never imagine that someone would disclose their HIV status. I did and I didn't feel awkward about it. I knew that if I was going to be putting myself on this dating website to find someone who I could potentially be spending the rest of my life with, I wanted to make sure they knew up front that I was HIV positive, that it was nothing to joke about, and that I wasn't one who hid it.

I registered to the site in February with a 3 month trial just to see if this was something that was worth it. After weeks of being on there I met quite a few guys. I decided to keep my searches local to Orlando. Of course men from all over found my profile and began messaging me. One of those men happened to be from Hollywood, FL and he works for Microsoft in the XBOX division. Now I've never had a preference in race, skin color, or anything like that, but most men I've been with were light skin or brown skin. This man right here was one of the most handsome chocolate men that I had ever met in my life. His skin was so damn near perfect to me. He was in his late 30's, and after chatting for days just on the website we decided to exchange numbers and I learned that he loved eating food that I would never eat. We finally met offline and met multiple times thereafter; on one of those occasions he bought and cooked me frog legs. Now if you know me, you know I don't eat chitterlings, so you know I wasn't about to try and eat those things. Well, I did! I was like, you know, how can I say what I don't like unless I try it, at least just one time. HATED IT! Maybe it was because they were not fried but they didn't taste like chicken to me.

That adventure lasted all of about 3 weeks because we both decided that it just wouldn't work out. He accepted my status and I accepted his strange eating habits, but he was also OCD so, being a heath nut and me being HIV positive, he'd always be crazy with going to the doctor and all kinds of stuff.

So now here I am at the end of March and its March 30$^{th}$. I was getting so fed up with this website. I had met so many wonderful men but they all were so very far away. I still had more of my free trial left but I didn't care. I went to the account setting page and, just as I was about to click to delete my account, a message popped up in my inbox. I said, "You know what, I'm going to do this one more time…" I went to my inbox and there was a message from a user named DJSAFETY. I immediately assumed that he was a DJ; I was into music and radio broadcasting so that was my initial thought. I then began to read his inbox message. Now, if you've been keeping up with me on FB, you'll remember me posting about keeping certain things from your past that you never realize would be relevant in the future. You guessed it! I saved our very first conversation. I'd love to share this with everyone:

March 31, 2013 12:34 PM

He Said: Hi I hope this email finds you smiling because you have a great smile. I'm sure you have been told that over and over. I welcome you to view my profile and see if maybe there is something you may find interesting or maybe you would like to just stop by and say hi. Either way I know that you will find that one person who will make you happy/loved.

I would enjoy possibly getting to know you if you're interested please ask any questions and I can promise to answer them truthfully.

Have a great night and great weekend

March 31, 2012 6:04 PM

You Said: Well have you read my entire profile and understood a major part of my life that I deal with? I appreciate your compliment. BTW I'm Renee' but mostly everyone calls me Byrd or LadyByrd....so DJ SAFETY? What's that name for do you DJ?

March 31, 2012 6:30 PM

He Said: I have gone back and read your entire profile....I look back at your photos, and I see someone so much stronger than myself. I would like to continue chatting with you, how can I resist with a smile like yours.lol

March 31, 2012 6:34 PM

You Said: you're a rare one that's for sure! So tell me how is your weekend going? If you like you can text me or call me 904-XXX-XXXX....I am back and forth watching TV lol

March 31, 2012 7:34 PM

He Said: Hey Byrd...I was preparing dinner for the kids and for me....everything came out okay...didn't burn the house down...lol I will store your number now and will text or call you

March 31, 2012 7:55 PM

You Said: ok great!

Reading that just now as I've share with you I feel that love at first chat moment all over again.

We immediately started talking and texting and I figured out that DJ SAFETY was his name and his occupation--- his name was DJ and he works as an Environmental Health and Safety Inspector. He lives in Brooklyn, NY and he's got 4 kids including a set of twins. I found that to be so amazing because we both had a boy and girl twin. Everything about our conversations and our life seemed to match so well. After a few weeks we decided that, although things would be long distance, we wanted a relationship and we make it happen.

Our next step was to officially meet. By now it was April and my birthday was nearing. He planned that he'd come and spend my birthday with me, and he did. Everything about my birthday weekend was so amazing. We went to downtown Orlando and walked around Lake Eola and just enjoyed each other and talked, looked at the swans, and took pictures. Our first OFFICAL picture together and we were so cute! This was on that Friday. Saturday we stayed home and we just enjoyed each other. We went shopping and decided to watch some movies and cook dinner. It was raining and my son was fast asleep. We just sat there looking out the window at the rain and talked. We talked about everything you can think of. No topic was left out and everything just felt so right. That night we ended up making love. I hadn't had sex in over a year so that night was everything to me. The sex was passionate and it was rough. We were so into the moment that we didn't realize that something happened. The condom broke.

...OK now before you get all in an uproar about the condom breaking let me break this down. I didn't know the condom broke and didn't find out until the next day. My birthday!

I woke up that morning to a kiss on the forehead. "Morning Honey" is what he said to me as his lips planted the gentlest kiss. I got up and he had my gifts laid out on the table for me to open. He had someone to make a custom keychain that had our pictures engraved in it and that lit up our favorite color of blue. I also got my favorite perfume that I just love, Clinique Happy, along with a perfume that I had sampled once called 'I Love NY'. I got dressed and we went to breakfast at Cracker Barrel. After that we spent the day at the mall. He took me on a shopping spree that included buying my dress, shoes, and jewelry that I would wear to dinner that night. I was in heaven! I had never felt so special in my life. I've had many dates, but nothing compared to the way he was making me feel.

That night we went out to my favorite restaurant, The Cheesecake Factory. He got a bottle of Moscato and I ordered whatever I wanted. By the time we got halfway through dinner we were both tipsy and snapping pictures and laughing. When they brought my birthday cake to the table I was so excited! They sang 'Happy Birthday' to me and he asked them to bring out some "extra" whipped cream. Let's just say that was a part of the to-go containers.

We got back home and I put Micah to sleep and got him settled. When I came back out of the room I was in shock! Candles were lit, music was playing, and the mood was so right. He grabbed me and we started dancing to the music. I felt like I was in a fairy tale movie. He was caressing my back, rubbing my arms from the shoulder to the finger tips. He took his finger and lifted my chin and this six foot three inches of a man leaned down and gave me the most passionate kiss. Grabbed me and picked me up like I was a feather and laid me down.

Before I knew anything we were engaging in sexual intercourse and without a condom. I immediately stopped him and asked him what he was doing? He said, "If I am your man and that I am, then I want you to give me all of you and I give you all of me." I asked him why he felt like that and he told me then that he had already exposed himself to me and my status and that the condom the night before had broken. I can completely admit that I was taken by the mood and we had unprotected sex. I ask myself after the fact did I allow the right thing to happen, and I even cried about it because God knows that I never in a million years want to be the reason that anyone becomes infected with the HIV virus.

It happened….No not that he got infected, but every time we saw each other and we engaged in sex it was unprotected. This man was in love with me and I was in love with him. He promised me that he was not going anywhere and I believed him!

Here it was June 13, 2012 and I was at the Jacksonville International Airport about to get aboard a JetBlue airplane heading to JFK airport in New York. I had never been on an airplane in my 29 years of life and I wasn't even scared. I was very excited about this experience that I was having. I talked on the phone with my honey until I had to turn my phone off and he reassured me that he would see me as soon as I landed. The sky was so beautiful and I could see why so many people loved to fly. I had my music playing and it was so serene. I was in the clouds literally. The flight was about 2 hours but it seemed like it was not that long. When we landed I went and got my luggage. He was there waiting on me to arrive and I jumped in his arms and got a huge kiss. We only saw each other once a month for anywhere from 3-5 days, and I had never been to New York to sightsee so this was going to be so relaxing. The entire time I was there we did so much stuff. I saw Coney Island, The Statue of Liberty, the 9-11 sites, and we just really enjoyed our time together.

The highlight of my trip was finally getting to meet my new found brother Julien. He and my slave Marlon (you must know the story) were in the area not too far from where DJ and I were at so we linked up and had a few drinks. We took a few pictures and had some good old laughs. For all my Julien O'Neal Facebook page family and friends, blame him for not having the "spades party" while I was in town!

I was not ready to leave New York at all. I wasn't ready to leave the man that I was madly in love with, the man that God sent to me. However I boarded my plane and was back in Florida alone. Two months went by and neither of us was able to make a trip to see each other. Work had him working doubles and he was sleeping and working and working and sleeping. Finally we made flight reservations for him to come to Florida for Me 'Kayla's birthday weekend on September 15$^{th}$. I had won 4 tickets to SeaWorld so we took her and her cousin for her birthday. That same weekend is the weekend that I think started the end of things.

Almost 2 weeks after that awesome weekend we had, I began to be sleepy, nauseous, and vomiting. I thought, "Come on, Renee', you can't be pregnant". I have 3 kids so I know the signs and symptoms but, like any woman, I got online and I searched for all the signs and symptoms. They all pointed to early pregnancy symptoms. I sucked it up and took a home pregnancy test, and I saw a VERY faint line. I went POAS crazy. I was so crazy that I was using pregnancy terms; POAS means 'Pee on a Stick'. Anyway I had already told him that I thought I was pregnant. I waited until I was to miss my next period and I took another test and this time it was definite. I was pregnant, and calculations put me at about 4 weeks. I immediately called doctors because I knew I had to stop taking the medication I was on because it can cause birth defects; one of the risks I knew when I agreed to take the medicine without any birth control involved.

I was excited because here I was about to take a journey down a road that not many people would be privileged to be able to let the world experience with them. I was an HIV Positive woman and I got pregnant from an HIV Negative man. How in the world did that happen? People wanted to know and for the first time I am admitting that I lied to a lot of people, even my own parents. How was I to explain to anyone that I willingly let this man have unprotected sex with me knowing that I could be infecting him. I was happy about the baby but ashamed about how it all happened. By now DJ and I had planned on getting married; months prior we set the date of March 31, 2014 in Barbados on the beach at sunset. We knew exactly what we wanted.

Now it was the end of October, and I was already somewhat showing. This scared me because I had dreams that I was pregnant with twins and I just knew it was twins again. DJ was home and I was so ready to be in his arms. I wanted him to hold me and rub my belly, something I never experienced with my other kids' father. Everything felt so right….until November 1, 2012. We made it back to Orlando after spending that weekend with the kids and taking them to the fair for Halloween. I got in the door and immediately had to use the bathroom, and when I pulled my panties down there was blood in the seat of them. I screamed and yelled out to DJ to come quick that something was wrong with the baby. I was in such a panic that I rushed to the ER to be checked out and I was told that spotting was normal and that it was too early to see the baby.

For 2 weeks I got the run around with ERs and doctors until finally I went to Winnie Palmer Hospital in Orlando. The doctor there informed me that I had a miscarriage called a Blighted Ovum. This type of miscarriage is when you start out developing all the hormones needed to support a fetus but, for whatever reason, the baby never grows at all. Your body does everything until it realizes that there is nothing there; that's when it starts to eliminate waste. I was given the option to take a pill, have a D&C, or to miscarry naturally; I chose to let things happen on its own. I miscarried for the entire month of November. That night I went home and I cried, I cried so hard that I fell asleep. The next day DJ and I talked like we did every day from the first day we met. We never missed a day without talking or telling each other how much we loved one another. He told me that we could always try again, that he was hurting just as bad as I was, and that he too had been crying.

I was not ready for what was about to happen to me. This moment is one that I just admitted to myself and my best friend today June 17, 2013 that I am still healing from.

It was now a week before Christmas, and like DJ did every time he got paid he made sure that if I needed help with anything he would send me some money. We were talking and he was checking his bank account; then, all of a sudden, he said he would call me back and that something was wrong with his bank account. I tried calling him the rest of that evening and all day Saturday and didn't get an answer. I decided that I'd try to call Sunday morning and that's when he answered. He said, "I know you want to talk to me and I want to explain what happened but my phone is going dead and I have to direct my uncle to my house". That was the last conversation I ever had with him and one last text that said he'd call me later. For the next two weeks I called, texted, emailed. I even called his supervisor at his job to make sure that everything was ok and she said that he had been coming to work like normal and she'd tell him to call me. I then knew that whatever was wrong with him was causing him to completely shut me out. The first thought that came to mind was that he had found out he was infected but then I thought, "No that couldn't be it because he would have told me." Plus he said he didn't worry about becoming infected being that we were going to spend the rest of our life together.

This then caused me to investigate, and I found that a week before we talked there was a court date where an old debt caught up with him, and the judge granted them an order them to garnish his bank account. This I could believe because, when he was about to send me the money, he said that something didn't look right in his account.

At that very moment I sent him this email:

I just want to know you're safe and that you still love me and the kids. I can't stop crying and I'm depressed not knowing what is going on is bothering me but I have to let you handle things your own way. It hurts me that you won't talk to me but I can be with you at your worst and damn sure be with you at your best. Whatever it is that's going on you don't even have to tell me. I just need to know that we're still in love like we have been since day one. Shutting me out the way you are is hurting me and the kids....I've been calling and texting but Me'Kayla keeps calling you from the house phone. I told her she won't reach you but she keeps trying. Just know that we love you and that we aren't going ANYWHERE! I PROMISE you that! No matter what it is! You are my heaven sent and when you're hurting so am I.....we have a special bond and connection that can't be broken. Whatever is hurting you so bad I will pray about it for you like I have been doing and I will give you your space and your time to heal or handle whatever it is. Just please let me at least know you still without a doubt love me and the kids.

---

Renee'

Your Wife!

I then sent another email telling him that if I didn't hear from him by January 1, 2013 then I was going into the new years alone and single. I had cried and cried and cried. I cried harder than I did when I had the miscarried. I was hurting, and from that moment I promised myself that I'd never let another man hurt me like that ever again.

After that email the New Year came and as I had said I went into the year of 2013 single and with new ventures on my agenda. I was planning on dealing with a few surgeries with my son and that involved being back in Jacksonville, FL for awhile. I also was planning on completing my book and getting it published. I only had a few more pages to write so I kept setting myself deadlines until I finally completed my book. Writing plus disabled children and trying to work all took a toll on me so I voluntarily quit working and focused on my kids and my book.

I am proud to present to you my all. With hard work, dedication, trials, and error I have completed a very much needed chapter in my life.

## Q&A

Every Tuesday on my Facebook page I ask people to inbox me questions that they want me to answer and I post those questions along with my answer on my wall for everyone to see. I make sure to keep all names anonymous. What I want to do is share those questions and my answers with you all. I am doing this so that if someone reads this book and has questions they just might find that long lost answer here. Please keep in mind when reading the questions that I also decided to keep all dialect, slang, and origination of the questions as is:

Q: This is my question.... what happened to your ex husband after he served jail? Did you forgive him?

A. He went back to live in Greenville, SC, YES he's been forgiven.

Q. What were some of the symptoms you developed before you were diagnosed with HIV? 2. Can you contract HIV from having sex once with a person that is infected? 3. How long did you and husband have sex before you tested positive (if it is too personal I understand)?

Thank you for doing this.

A. I never had any symptoms. Most people who are HIV positive NEVER experience any symptoms.

You are at risk ANYTIME you engage in unprotected sex with anyone who could have anything.

Our first time having unprotected sex was our wedding night and that was Aug 2007 I was diagnosed Nov 2007

Q: I want to be open about my situation but my boyfriend is worried about how his family and mostly how his kids are going to feel because they've already been hearing rumors and they don't want him to be with me. I cried myself to sleep last night because I don't know what to do. Feels like I'm stuck between a rock and a hard place! Any advice?

A. I will say this in the nicest way possible. SCREW HIM AND HIS KIDS! If he is afraid to be with you and you want to be open about your status then guess what he needs to be alone and you need to move on to bigger and better things. Don't let any man keep you from doing what you want to do. OK so you've cried last night...now I want you to hold your head up and now you must make a decision. ONLY you can make it but you have to decide if you're going to live YOUR life or the life someone else wants you to live.

Q. Is it true that it's hard for a guy to catch HIV from a female because she would have

to come to pass the virus

A. Partially incorrect. True it's hard for a woman to pass HIV to a man but it's not impossible. False when you say a female would have to climax to pass the virus. Anytime you have unprotected sex you're at risk! Whether either person "cums" or not.

Q. Did your husband ever say why he did it?

A. He told me and the judge when asked under oath that he didn't tell me he had it because he didn't want me to leave him. That everyone who he's ever told left him and he didn't want me to leave. The judge said "well sir what did she do? She left....and now you're going to jail!"

Q. would you have taken your x husband back after he got out of jail, if you felt like he was truly sorry, being as you forgave him or was forgiving him more just about your own personal sanity?

A. Before he went into jail and while married to me he was with another woman whom he got pregnant. While in jail he remained with her and when he got out of jail he went to be with her. I divorced him while he was incarcerated. I never had any intentions of EVER remaining with him. Sorry or not my trust was broken and will probably never be regained by him.

Q: I know you deal with a lot on a daily basis, but I want you to know I admire you sooo much and I appreciate what you did for my baby. Lord knows I do! But my question is HOW ARE YOU? HOW IS RENEE DOING?

A. your son is just so adorable and I don't mind helping anyone who needs help.

I am doing well. I won't say great because I'd be lying but I'm still here and that's what matters to me. Went to the Dr. today and all my labs were good with the exception of my blood sugar. I'm working it all out. I have those good and bad days but the good always over powers the bad.

Q. Hi you may have answered this question already... But what happened to your twins?

A. My twins were born 4 months premature and both have developmental delays all non-related to my HIV status. They are both HIV Negative.

Q. Since you flooding my timeline answering all these damn questions. Answer my question on your wall...Ain't I Da Coolest Swaggered Out Supa Swervtastic Nucca (Paula Dean Vc) You Know? And Would You Be Mad If I Smacked Fie Out Ur Ex If I Ever Saw Him For Thinking He Could Defeat A Child Of GOD Wit HIV? And Don't He Know You Serve An Almighty Power?

A. Well hello Hater #2 lol.....I guess you got a lil swagger. I wouldn't be mad I know how much it pissed you off. If he doesn't know "HE GONE LEARN TODAY!"

Q. Ur so beautiful and strong and I love that about u....... you're not letting the devil still your joy. ? Are you dating? How do men react to you when you tell them? Are you back in Jacksonville, fl?

A. Thanks! The devil won't win over here! I am in the process of learning someone. Not sure if I should call it dating or what. Men react strange but in a good way. You'd be completely surprised at how many men are attracted to me even while knowing my status. I don't know if it's my openness that does it but hey....I still got it! LOL Thought I was gonna have to do like Stella to get my groove back and stuff. I am in Jacksonville not sure for how long. My son has been having alot of surgery which sparked my return.

Q. Even though u said u have no contact with ur ex husband, do u think he's still sleeping around spreading the disease after he has already served his time?

In an excerpt from ur book when u stated that u told his sister u wasn't n town when she arrived and u told her why. Does u still talk to his sister?

A. I don't know if he's still doing it. His face was all over TV in SC but we all know how most young adults Don't Watch the news who's to say he hasn't found a young naive one to infect.

I don't talk to her. She is VERY messy and I will not have a middle person that I confide in and she goes back and twist things around. I mailed her pics of her niece and nephew and that's it.

<u>Inbox motivation:</u> Hello ms Renee I don't know you but I see you posting a lot of things and I just wanted to take the time out to tell you thank you for being you and letting everybody know that this can happen very easy you influence me a lot to go and get checked every couple of months I can't imagine what you are goin thru because I'm not in your position but may god bless you and keep you near him I will keep you in my prayers I might not know you but you touched my heart and a very strong women I can see that and I know you not afraid so keep your head up you didn't ask for none of this all you wanted to do was be loved the respectful right way

<u>Inbox Motivation:</u> I'm so glad 2 knw sumbdy lik u even tho alotta years have passed since high school...lol when i seen u on a commercial instantly i was shocked cudnt believe it actually was hoping u where jst a actor...but after i added u on fb & seen how open u r im proud.

Q. U not only embraced ur circumstance but u have also helped alotta people... I always said sumthing like that wud break me so my question is... Has there eva been a time when u thought u just wanted to give up on life due to ur status??

A. I have had suicidal thoughts before but that's just what it was THOUGHTS you'd be scared f I told you just how recent my last thought was....It happens but I have so much faith that I'd never let myself result to that.

Q. Do you ever wish other women were more open about the chance of getting it from a husband, or the media seeming to of hidden this for many years and only concentrating on gay or drug use as being the major focus of how to get this horrible disease. Would someone speaking out before have changed how you went about your relationship? I know I regret not speaking up many years ago at times but I was just not strong enough so sometimes I feel guilty even though I know I can’t control what others do, but sometimes I wonder if I did speak up like I had been asked if it might of made a huge difference or not.

A. I do wish that they were. People think that marriage means safety and it doesn't. I was educated on HIV and AIDS so I wouldn't have changed how I went about my relationship. I was in love and we all know love can blind you from signs. It's called living life. But alot of people don't live life safe and aware they are naive and free. It's OK to be free but be safe too. Speaking out for me makes a huge impact on my life. I couldn't image not telling anyone and living in darkness.

Q. I know that you said originally you had no symptoms. Do you have any now? Is it true that the meds make you feel worse?

A. I still have no symptoms. The meds all have various side effects so it's just all about each individual person and how their body reacts.

Inbox Motivation: I think u r the most awesome person I know...I mean I really don't know u but fr u r wonderful I been goin thru some things an I thgt I was at da bottom in my life ...but lookn at yo page an reading some of yo stuff ....an I realize if u goin thru dos things an still smile y cant I ......I RESPECT U TO DA UPMOST FR FR.....

Q. First off I would like to applaud you for not only being open, but opening your life to others to help them. My question is would you think it's wrong to start a web site with the information and pictures of people who knowingly infect people?

A. Thank you. As far as your idea of a website, if you want to be sued by someone who probably should be in jail then I wouldn't do it. By law you can not disclose anyone's medical status of any kind. That can result in a slander or defamation suit again you or whoever does it.

Q. Hi, have it ever crossed your mind that the Majority of these people that are questioning you are actually infected themselves?

A. Most people confide in me so I know who is and who isn't and that doesn't even matter. What matters is that they are asking and seeking help and advice.

Q. Is it true that there is no scientific evidence that proves HIV causes AIDS? And is it true that once ur diagnosed with HIV you don't have to start treatment until your t cells get below a certain number?

A. In my opinion there had to be scientific proof because when it was first discovered it was only known as AIDS and through lots of research and studying they found that it was not just AIDS but the stage of HIV existed.

Your T-cells along with your viral load determine whether you are put on meds. Some people have a strong immune system and their body can fight and regulate those levels but if your t-cells are say 269 which is over 200 (under 200 is AIDS) and your viral load is say 13,000 copies most likely you'll be put on meds because you have thousands of replicating HIV cells in your body.

Inbox Motivation: Morning, I just had to tell you that you are AMAZING... Please keep inspiring people and most importantly please continue to KEEP it REAL... God has place such an awesome calling on your life... I thank you for not being ashamed to tell your story.... Many blessings to you and your family...

---

Q. Hey Renee good morning I have a question I kno it might sound stupid I had sex with this guy we used a condom but then he took it off we had unprotected sex for like 3min then I told him to stop he didn't cum or anything my question is can I get HIV from that.

A. Sadly yes you can still become infected. It only takes a few seconds of exposure to be potentially infected.

Q. Is day to day difficult or just at times if any? Also, is pos & neg status sexual relationships common & how are they maintained? You are so beautiful by the way & very strong

A. Just some days are harder than others and it's not a physical thing it's more mental.

It's very common and it's maintained just as any relationship with all the values anyone else wants and deserves in a relationship. Sex is treated as any should be treated...PROTECTED!

Q. Honestly speaking, but I know how a lot of people are just real life social butterflies and take to people very well, but my question is...Do you think you would normally have this much love in your life had you not opened up so many eyes because of your story? Do you get what I'm trying to say? Lol didn't know how to really word this

A. I get what you're saying and yes! I come from a very large family and it's full of love I have over 100 cousins. So if I never had the love and support from friends and associates and strangers I'd still have tons of love from family.

Q. Good morning the Times when u get depressed or can't sleep because of your situation what do u do to help you?

A. I used to drink.....alot. I started in 2008 drinking almost every night just so I could fall asleep and then July 2010 I went cold turkey and I didn't touch another drink for almost 2 years.....I then started occasional drinking like maybe when I'd go out to dinner or something. Now I just recently had to stop completely because of my diabetic pill. So I do what I should have done before I started drinking and that was talk to my God in prayer until I fell asleep.

Q. not to sound like a typical male but being human and having sexual desires but with you being HIV positive are you still able to have a normal sex life?

Don't mean to get so personal sorry if I offended you

A. No Offense taken. I do still have a normal sex life. People think HIV means no sex.

Q. Hi it's always hard for me to achieve a orgasm it takes a long time it only happens maybe out of 10 times 1 time is it something I'm doing wrong?

A. For those who will wonder this Questions is from a female. There could be alot of factors to consider. Age can be one of the main ones along with your hormonal balance. It could very well be the man who you're having sex with not knowing how to hit those spots that will make you have that orgasm you're longing for. I personally would mention this to my Dr. Especially if you're not over the age of 40. There could very well be a medical explanation for it.

Q. Would u consider HPV and HIV sorta the same since it is virus and the body has to fight it off it can turn into cancer and to me Cancer is worse than HIV whats ur opinion about that

A. I think all diseases are horrible. Even with Cancer you can still have sex unprotected if you want. HPV is considered and STD which can cause genital warts and Cancer so I mean kind of the same but very different in more ways.

Q. Good morning, if you are HIV positive can you be a donor and not pass it to someone else...what I mean is can your level be so low that you can be just a carrier and not pass it to your mate..

A. It's possible to have HIV and not pass it to anyone else and if you're undetectable there is a 1% chance of passing it.

Q. Ok you don't have to post this if you don't want to, but do you still receive oral sex? (Too invasive?)

A. Yes I do. With the use of a protective barrier.

---

Q. When first meeting someone, talking/dating so you tell them about the HIV right away? Or wait awhile. How have people reacted from you being honest and telling them...? Btw you and your babies are very beautiful!! & you are beyond a strong woman, I salute you honey!

A. I tell them right away. If they ask me for my number I tell them and let them choose to still give me their number or not. People are always shocked at my honesty. Thanks so much for the motivational words

Q. So the people with the strong immune system don't have to take anti retro viral pills because there viral load is high but they are still detectable right because the pills are to stop the spread of the virus Idk if I said it right

A. No if your viral load is High you will need to take the medicine. If your T-Cells (CD4 Count) are over 200 and in good marginal range and your viral load is undetectable without meds they more than likely won't put you on them. High viral Loads cause your CD4 counts to decrease because the HIV attacks those T-cells which are your T-helper cells that help fight off infection.

Inbox Motivation: First I want to let you know that you are a blessing to so many people out here. I'm sorry that you are going through this but God has your back. I contracted the virus from birth and I thank God everyday for holding on to me all these years because it's only because of Him I am here today even when the doctors said I wouldn't live to see the age of two. You are very strong and amazing and beautiful and you inspire me as well as others. My sister, keep up the good work.

Q. Will HIV turn into aids?

A. Yes if the person decides that what their doctor says is best for them to do they don't want to do. Like take their medicine. It's all about keeping your immune system healthy.

Acknowledgements

It took me a few years but I did it! I wrote this book like I said I would. I have so many people to thank but first and foremost I have to give my God all the honor, glory, and praise. For all those times I felt that I had carried enough heavy burdens he showed me that I was way much stronger than I could have ever imagined. To my kids Me'Kayla, Michelle, and Micah because if not got them I'd probably be gone from this earth having never told my story and changed lives. My parents for teaching me all that I know that has help mold me into the woman I am today at 30 years old. For all those who have made an impact in my life over the years.

To those who contributed to making this book possible to be published and assisting me with getting my story out to the world I thank you a million times over.

My parents and kids Ruth, Johnny II, Me'Kayla, Michelle, and Micah…..

Johnny & Anesha Burgess

Ben Stuart

Jillian Moody

Damon Nicholson

NaTarsha Thomas

Erika Davidson

Kharisma Ewing & Dew Family

Sharika Thornes

Christie Shelton

Kim Thrower-Morgan

Timothy Upson

Patricia Symonds-Powell

Rashell Middleton

Janna Saia

Carley Rudd

Angela Sherrer

Toccara Richardson

Evelyn Jones

Monica Brown

Lisa Hill-Prier

Darralyn Cody

LaTeena Hubbard

Tamura Davis

Mashanna Tucker

Rob Anderson

Patricia Thomas

Jewel Walker-Terrell

Lamnette Douglas

Miriam J. Barnett

Jamie Henderson

Alysha Townsend

Monica Bradley

Tionna Alford

Russia Hunter

Jawandayln Johnson

Shontell Cook

Charlotte Singleton

Eddie & Nicole Boston

LaKiesha Brown-Scott

Phadra Pinckney

Jennifer Williams

Shanel Shotomiwa

Timothy Mobley

LaKeisha Everett

Laron Burns

Antoinette Upkins

Darryl Wright

Lyric Robinson

Kris Jones

Norma Jaimez

Kim Hunter

Erika Thomas

Martha Sanchez

Angela Scully

Daric Williams

Angelica Iniquez

Delores Ray- In Memory of Shawn Ray

Candice Hammond

Dana M. Johnston

Michael Jackson

Brenda Williams

Mckenzi Kids.Net

Byron Shields

Joaquin Evans

Kendall McCray

Keith Reid

Ingrid Watkins

Terrence Mason

Latasha Richardson

Abeni Kelley

James Harris

Terra Green

Marquita Butler

Precious Holmes

Willis Johnson

Shawn Davis

Aquina Moses

Shenette Pierce

Latoya Warren

Dr. Jennifer Chally

Larry & Cathy Byers

Julien O'Neal

Shawna Williams

Lakisha Jordan

Courtney Bankhead

Mark Hicks

Katrina General

Erika Gaffney

Shante Brown

Crystal Rakauckas

Keisha Hyndman

Stacy Robb

Nadine Woodburn

Anita Sumlin

Nacole Dickens

Tara Bullock

Clifford Mapp, Jr.

Quin Jones

Kashia Cannon

Richard Beavers

Desaree Cason

Christopher Carson

Travis Dowlen

Patrick Anglade

Deborah Williams

Margeaux Kimberly Blue

Natasha Jenkins

Simone Walker

The Love Jones Experience

Julia Abney

Tiffany Oliver

Larry Key

Patricia Williams

Gina Berger

Latoya Dotson

Tisa Morris-Christian

Karlita Johnson

Claude Graham

Felecia Williams

Darryl Polite

Black Women DO Workout

Stephanye Hudson

Danielle Williams

David Whiters

Vicki Hoard

Aisha Snipes-Gilzene

Monica Jennings

www.ingramcontent.com/pod-product-compliance
Lightning Source LLC
LaVergne TN
LVHW091010080826
845145LV00003B/1212

* 9 7 8 0 6 1 5 8 6 1 6 0 9 *